D1315588

GENETIC DISEASES
AND GENE THERAPIES

MULTIPLE SCLEROSIS

Richard Spilsbury

rosen publishing's
**rosen
central**

New York

Published in 2019 by The Rosen Publishing Group, Inc.
29 East 21st Street
New York, NY 10010

Copyright © 2019 by The Rosen Publishing Group, Inc.

First Edition

All rights reserved. No part of this book may be reproduced in any form without permission in writing from the publisher, except by a reviewer.

Produced for Rosen by Calcium Creative Ltd
Editors for Calcium: Sarah Eason and Kris Hirschmann
Designer: Simon Borrough
Picture researcher: Rachel Blount

Photo credits: Cover: Shutterstock: Blackboard: bottom right; Borysevych.com: main; Andrii Muzyka: bottom; Inside: Shutterstock: Africa Studio: pp. 17, 27; Alpa Prod: pp. 20, 34; Peter Bernik: p. 33; Phichet Chaiyabin: p. 13b; CKP1001: p. 28; Designua: pp. 8, 9, 42; Dean Drobot: pp. 6, 47; Janson George: p. 37; HelloRF ZcooL: p. 18; Neenawat Khenyothaa: p. 41; Stanislaw Mikulski: p. 15; NadyaEugene: p. 14; Nejron Photo: p. 31; Tyler Olson: p. 40; Jarun Ontakrai: p. 13t; Elena Pavlovich: p. 39; Atthapon Raksthaput: p. 21; Ralwel: p. 5; Ranjith Ravindran: p. 36; Realpeople: p. 35; Spreewald.picture.de: p. 11; Tyler Stuard: pp. 24-25; Jenny Sturm: p. 45; Yakobchuk Viacheslav: p. 23; Li Wa: p. 22; Tom Wang: p. 29; Wavebreakmedia: p. 4; Wikimedia Commons: DIAC images: p. 10.

Cataloging-in-Publication Data

Names: Spilsbury, Richard.
Title: Multiple sclerosis / Richard Spilsbury.
Description: New York : Rosen Central, 2019. | Series: Genetic diseases and gene therapies | Includes glossary and index.
Identifiers: LCCN ISBN 9781508182849 (pbk.) | ISBN 9781508182832 (library bound)
Subjects: LCSH: Multiple sclerosis--Juvenile literature.
Classification: LCC RC377.S646 2019 | DDC 616.8'34--dc23

Manufactured in the United States of America

Contents

Chapter 1
What Is Multiple Sclerosis?

Have you ever felt exhausted after a long hike, or so numb in the legs after sitting cross-legged for a while that you cannot walk, or dizzy after getting off an amusement park ride? Have you ever felt a sudden desperation to use the toilet, or stumbled over your speech? Some people may feel or experience all of these things together most of the time, along with pain, intolerance to heat, and many other symptoms. They feel this way because they have multiple sclerosis.

Nervous System

People with multiple sclerosis experience so many varied symptoms around the body because it is a disease affecting their nervous system. The nervous system is a network of nerves in our bodies that carry information to and from the body's control center—the brain. Information comes from outside the body via the senses of touch, taste, hearing, vision, and smell. Information also comes from internal organs such as the stomach, that may be empty and need food, or the bladder, that may be full and need to be emptied. Peripheral nerves around the body connect with the spinal cord tucked safely away in the spine.

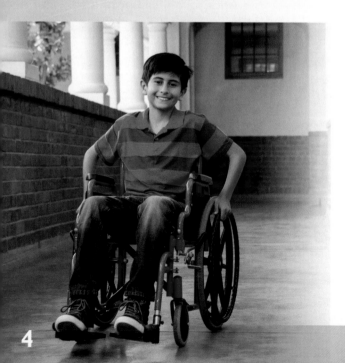

Having multiple sclerosis is challenging and life-altering. But its symptoms can often be controlled and lessened so people with this disorder can live full and happy lives.

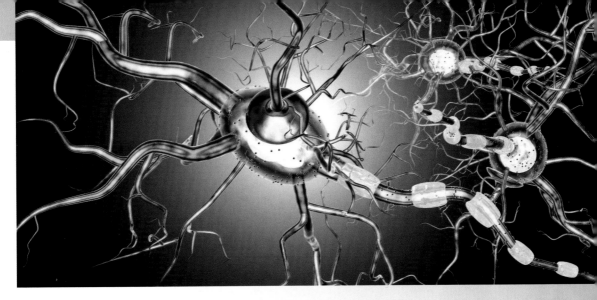

The symptoms of multiple sclerosis are the result of physical abnormalities of neurons, or nerve cells, in the nervous system.

The spinal cord is around eighteen inches (46 cm) long and up to half an inch (1.3 cm) thick, and it is the superhighway of the nerve world. It funnels information speedily and directly toward and away from the brain so it can communicate with the body. Millions of neurons in the brain send signals throughout the body to control movement, sensation, memory, understanding, and speech. Every time you take a step, blink, or move your arm, your brain and spinal cord are at work, together forming the central nervous system (CNS). Multiple sclerosis happens when neurons in the CNS become damaged so they cannot carry out their normal work. Because multiple sclerosis affects nerves, we say that it is a neurological disease.

Widespread Disease

Globally, around 2.3 million people have multiple sclerosis. People do not catch the disease or inherit it directly through their genes. Many factors, including the infections they have, their genes, and even where they are from, all help to determine whether they get the disease. Multiple sclerosis is a progressive disease because it usually worsens over time. Its course is unpredictable because symptoms vary widely from person to person. Symptoms can improve or periodically become worse through a person's life.

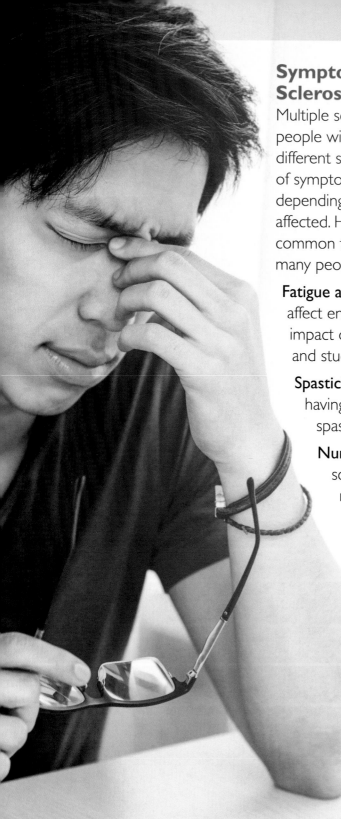

Symptoms and Types of Multiple Sclerosis

Multiple sclerosis is highly variable. Two people with the disorder may have very different signs and symptoms. Their range of symptoms can also change over time, depending where their nerves are being affected. However, some symptoms are more common than others and are experienced by many people with multiple sclerosis.

Fatigue and weakness: These symptoms affect energy levels, which can have an impact on a person's ability to work and study.

Spasticity: This means feeling stiff and having uncontrolled muscle twitches or spasms, most commonly in the legs.

Numbness or tingling: Multiple sclerosis may cause a person to feel numbness in the face, body, or limbs.

Dizziness: This is when someone feels unbalanced or light-headed, as though they are about to collapse.

Optic neuritis is one symptom of multiple sclerosis. This condition is characterized by temporary blurred vision, pain in eye movement, and even blindness. It happens when neurons in the optic nerve fail to work properly.

Walking difficulties: This symptom results from weakness in leg and feet muscles, dizziness affecting balance, numbness in the feet, and spasticity.

Pain: More than half of all people with multiple sclerosis feel the sensation of pain in their bodies, even when there is no direct stimulus to cause it.

Bladder and bowel problems: People with multiple sclerosis often experience incontinence and constipation.

Emotional and cognitive changes: People may experience strong mood swings, depression and other emotional changes, and/or a changing ability to process and learn information or focus attention.

Along with these common symptoms, people may also experience less-frequent symptoms such as slurred speech, problems swallowing or breathing, headaches, itching, and seizures.

Types of Multiple Sclerosis

Most people with multiple sclerosis experience symptoms over days or weeks, followed by periods of remission during which symptoms get better. Then they may have further relapses of previous symptoms or experience new symptoms. This pattern is called relapsing-remitting multiple sclerosis. Around two-thirds of the people with relapsing-remitting multiple sclerosis experience shorter remission periods and symptoms that gradually become worse. This pattern is called secondary-progressive multiple sclerosis. A smaller number of people experience continuous symptoms with no remissions. This pattern is called primary-progressive multiple sclerosis.

GENE STORIES

"My life with multiple sclerosis is an adventure where symptoms come and go, like running into many booby traps and obstacles. I can't make multiple sclerosis go away because it is part of my life, but it can't control me. I work hard at remaining positive, setting attainable goals, and constantly readjusting so I can live the best life I can and be the best version of me that I can be."

—*Daphne, age thirty-three*

Neuron Damage

Multiple sclerosis means "many scars." It was given that name because doctors examining patients with the disease spotted visibly hardened scar areas, or plaques, dotted through their CNS. Plaques are caused by damage to neurons or, more specifically, to an important substance called myelin that coats them.

The Importance of Myelin

If you have ever seen telephone cables, you may have noticed that they are thin and covered with plastic sleeves. An electric current runs through the cable's inner metal core. The plastic is an insulating material that stops the signal from escaping through the sides. If it escaped, it could lose information or slow down its transmission speed. Myelin around the axon, the long fiber part of a neuron, has the same job. It allows a nerve to pass electrical impulses rapidly to the next neuron without losing the signal. In the CNS, efficient impulses allow effortless, speedy, uninterrupted, and coordinated movements through the body. When myelin is lost from CNS neurons, however, impulses get disrupted. In turn, information to and from the brain and to muscles and other tissues can become garbled. This botched transmission causes the many symptoms of multiple sclerosis.

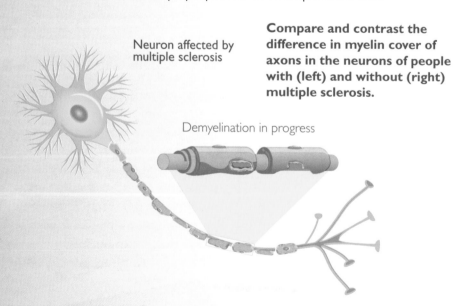

Neuron affected by multiple sclerosis

Compare and contrast the difference in myelin cover of axons in the neurons of people with (left) and without (right) multiple sclerosis.

Demyelination in progress

Attackers

Multiple sclerosis is said to be an immune-mediated disease because it is caused by the immune system. In a properly functioning immune system, white blood cells move to infection locations and gobble up invading bacteria and viruses so they do not cause further damage to the body. Sometimes, however, people have disorders in which the immune system changes its behavior and starts to attack normal healthy cells in the body rather than invaders. Multiple sclerosis is one such disorder.

In multiple sclerosis, T-cells and other white blood cells start to attack and destroy myelin on CNS neurons. They also attack cells near neurons called oligodendrocytes, which are myelin factories for axons. Plaques in the CNS result from such immune attacks. Their location affects the symptoms they cause. For example, plaques in the part of the spinal cord nearest the legs may affect walking, but those in the speech center of the brain may have an effect on a person's ability to speak clearly.

In relapsing-remitting multiple sclerosis, oligodendrocytes can recover between waves of immune attack and recoat neurons with myelin. Then plaques can heal and symptoms can go away. However, repeated attacks in the same places can eventually wipe out oligodendrocytes and even damage axons stripped of myelin. In progressive forms of the disease, permanent plaques may remain that affect brain activity and can even stop whole nerves from working, permanently affecting movements and body functions.

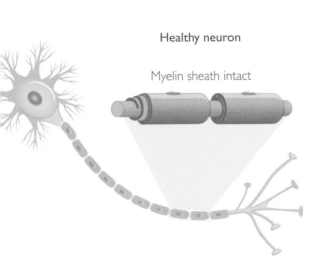

Healthy neuron

Myelin sheath intact

Who Develops Multiple Sclerosis?

Anyone can develop multiple sclerosis when their immune system goes out of control. Although the disorder can strike at any age, it most commonly erupts between fifteen and sixty years of age. However, scientists called epidemiologists looked at the backgrounds and medical histories of people with multiple sclerosis. They noticed patterns in the spread of the disease among the global population. Where you are from, your ethnic group, and your gender appear to make a difference in whether you will develop multiple sclerosis.

Climate

Multiple sclerosis is generally more common in people who live farther from the equator. This is the imaginary central horizontal line around our planet where temperatures are highest, on average. Points on the equator receive the sun's direct rays. The frequency of the disease increases heading north or south from the equator, into areas with cooler temperatures, less sunlight, and shorter summers.

Your ethnic background has an impact on whether you are likely to develop multiple sclerosis.

Ethnic Group and Origin

An ethnic group is often defined as people with shared ancestral, social, and even physical characteristics, often from particular areas in the world. Some ethnic groups have a lower- or higher-than-normal risk of developing multiple sclerosis. For example, many Sami and Inuit people traditionally live inside the Arctic circle, far from the equator, yet have low risk of developing the disease. Multiple sclerosis is virtually unheard of in Australian Aborigines. Some people, such as Parsis of India and Palestinians, live near the equator, yet have a higher-than-normal risk of developing multiple sclerosis. In general, people of northern European origin are at a slightly higher risk than people of Asian, Native American, or African descent.

In general, women living in more northerly regions are more likely to develop multiple sclerosis than men living nearer to the equator.

Gender

If you are female, then you have at least twice the risk that a male has of developing multiple sclerosis. Some scientists believe that hormonal differences may be a reason for this, especially since the disease usually shows up after puberty, when there are great hormonal changes in girls.

Gene Genies

A 2014 study found a clue to why more women than men develop multiple sclerosis. Researchers found that females susceptible to multiple sclerosis produce higher levels of a protein called S1PR2 than males do. They also found that the highest levels of that protein are found in areas of the brain that are usually damaged by multiple sclerosis. The protein helps control whether immune cells move from blood vessels into the brain. With more protein, more cells invade the brain and cause more inflammation and myelin damage.

Chapter 2

What Causes Multiple Sclerosis?

When someone gets bitten by a mosquito carrying a malaria parasite, they will usually develop a disease called malaria, which brings on dangerous fevers. When someone breathes in Mycobacterium bacteria, they will often develop the lung disease tuberculosis (TB). In both cases, the disease has a clear cause. However, multiple sclerosis is a bit different because several factors may be involved in causing the disorder, and the factors may interact in complicated ways. Scientists are researching the causes of multiple sclerosis in the hope of finding better ways to treat the disease.

Infections

Scientists suspect that some infections can cause multiple sclerosis. From birth, when bacteria or viruses enter our bodies, they attack cells. Our bodies normally trigger an immune response to the attacks. White blood cells eat the invaders and also produce antibodies. Antibodies are proteins that have a chemical that is made to fight a chemical on those specific invaders. Antibodies can damage or destroy invaders. They can also help bodies recognize the threat so it can be dealt with more easily during any future attacks.

Scientists have found that antibodies to some viruses and bacteria are found in larger amounts in people with multiple sclerosis than in people without the disease. Several possible viruses and bacteria may contribute to the development of multiple sclerosis, including the measles virus and pneumonia bacteria. But the most likely are:

Mono Virus: Mononucleosis, or mono, is often called the "kissing" disease due to the way it often spreads among younger people. It is actually caused by the Epstein-Barr virus, or EBV. EBV infection is

EBV is the virus responsible for mono infections and is also linked to developing multiple sclerosis.

characterized by fatigue, rash, fever, sore throat, swollen neck glands, and other symptoms. Antibodies to EBV are a lot higher in people with multiple sclerosis, indicating that they have been exposed to the disease. It therefore appears that being infected with mono increases the risk of having multiple sclerosis. Because the tiny virus hides out in the human body, the risk persists for several decades.

Human herpes virus 6 (HHV-6): The term HHV-6 actually refers to two closely related viruses: HHV-6A and HHV-6B. The B form infects nearly everyone on Earth, usually before the age of three, and usually causes mild fever, diarrhea, and a rash called roseola. The A form is rarer. Both types stay in people, doing nothing for long periods of time after initial infection. They sometimes cause health problems later on. HHV-6A is a trigger for relapses of multiple sclerosis. One study found that levels of its antibody were three times higher in women with progressive multiple sclerosis, too.

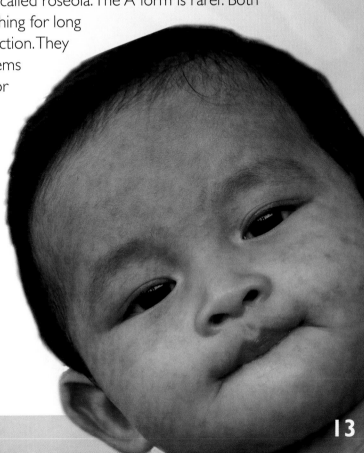

Skin rashes are one outward sign of several viral infections, including measles.

Environmental Factors

The environment we live in can have a big effect on our lives and health. For example, living in a home where someone smokes can increase the chances of having lung and heart problems. Epidemiologists have concluded that various environmental factors, from smoke exposure to sunlight levels, can contribute to the development of multiple sclerosis.

Sunlight and Vitamin D

One essential vitamin is vitamin D. It helps our bodies to absorb food nutrients such as calcium, and supports our immune responses. Most of our vitamin D is produced naturally in the skin when it is exposed to sunlight. People who live closer to the equator are exposed to greater amounts of sunlight all year. They have higher levels of natural vitamin D than people farther from the equator. Children and teenagers with low vitamin D have an increased risk of developing multiple sclerosis in later life. This effect has also been found in newborns, suggesting that vitamin D levels in a mother during pregnancy might affect a child's future risk of multiple sclerosis. Children born in the northern hemisphere in May are in early development inside their mothers during the darkest, lowest vitamin D times of year. Mothers of children born in November are exposed to more sunlight at a critical time of their pregnancy. So children born in May have a greater risk than children born in November.

Exposure to sunlight increases levels of vitamin D, helping to reduce the likelihood of developing multiple sclerosis.

Smoking can increase the chances of having multiple sclerosis and speed its progression.

Migration

Families and individuals migrate for many reasons, such as escaping danger or abuse, or seeking better work. Several studies have shown that when people younger than fifteen years of age migrate from a sunny region to a less-sunny region, they gain a higher risk of developing multiple sclerosis. The opposite is true of teenagers born in a high-risk area moving to a low-risk, sunnier place. If migration happens after age fifteen, a person's risk of developing multiple sclerosis does not change.

Unlikely Causes

Scientists have learned that some environmental factors are very unlikely to cause multiple sclerosis. For example, people living in places polluted with heavy metals, such as lead, may show the shaking and weakness typical of multiple sclerosis. However, they do not have the same overall symptoms, and there is no evidence that exposure to heavy metals causes multiple sclerosis. There is no evidence, either, that having allergies, having a dog, eating artificial sweeteners, or suffering physical trauma, can make people develop multiple sclerosis.

Genetic Factors

Some diseases, such as cystic fibrosis, are inherited. This means that people can only develop cystic fibrosis if their parents pass on the genes that cause it. This is not true of multiple sclerosis. However, people can still inherit genes that make it more likely they might develop the disease.

Genes

Genes store coded instructions that tell cells to make proteins which affect everything from the color of your hair to how you grow and your health. Every cell in our bodies contains a complete set of these instructions as sequences of chemicals, which are stored in the chromosomes in cells. Each gene in a chromosome has specialized sequence patterns providing the code to do particular jobs. Male sex cells (sperm) and female sex cells (ova, or eggs) each contain just one copy of each chromosome, or twenty-three chromosomes in total. During sexual reproduction, a sperm fertilizes or joins with an egg and the chromosomes of both pair up to make forty-six in the developing baby. During this process, slight variations in sequences can occur that cause the baby to have subtly different genes from its parents. Usually such mutations are not a problem, but sometimes genetic changes can have an impact on health.

Gene Genies

In 2016, Canadian scientists examining seven patients with multiple sclerosis from two unrelated families found that both carried the same gene mutation. Normal copies of the NR1H3 gene produce a protein called LXRA which helps to control inflammation of cells and tissues, and helps in the production of myelin. Having the variant makes multiple sclerosis more likely. Other scientists are unsure whether the NR1H3 variant is a major cause, since it is also found in people without the disease. However, the Canadian scientists believe this variant may make someone more likely to develop the disease than people who have the normal version.

If one identical twin has a higher-than-normal risk of multiple sclerosis, then his or her twin also has this risk, since they have the same genes.

Increased Risk

People who have a parent with multiple sclerosis have a 2 percent higher risk of developing the disease than someone in the normal population. The risk rises to 5 percent if they have a sibling with the disease and 30 percent if they have an identical twin with the disease. This is because of the genes they have inherited in common. These people might live completely normal lives. But they might also experience changes to their immune systems because of environmental factors that trigger the mutations. If this occurs, they progress to developing multiple sclerosis.

Chapter 3

Diagnosing Multiple Sclerosis

When a patient gets sick, health care workers must figure out which disease or condition explains the patient's symptoms and medical history. This is called making a diagnosis. Some conditions are easy to diagnose. However, because multiple sclerosis can cause so many symptoms, diagnosing this condition is not always simple.

When doctors hear of a possible multiple sclerosis symptom in a patient, they should investigate other signs and check the patient's medical history closely for episodes of health changes that may suggest the disease.

Consultations

Nearly one-third of patients eventually diagnosed with multiple sclerosis first visit their doctor with just one thing they are concerned about. This is often a change in their senses, such as blurred vision, a problem seeing colors, or eye pain typical of optic neuritis. Others may be worried about weakness or loss of sensation in one side of the body, lack of coordination causing them to drop things, or episodes of incontinence. If there are several symptoms typical of multiple sclerosis, a doctor might suspect the disease, even if the symptoms come and go. The doctor will then recommend more tests with specialists.

The next appointment is often with a neurologist, which is a doctor who is a specialist in nervous system problems. During a neurological examination, the doctor will ask the patient questions about past symptoms to establish a medical history. The neurologist may test for changes in eye movements, senses, limb coordination, balance, reflexes, or speech. Depending on the results, the neurologist may suspect multiple sclerosis even more strongly, and may order clinical tests to confirm the diagnosis.

Clinical Tests for Multiple Sclerosis

To be able to treat an illness safely and effectively, it is important to know rather than to guess the exact cause of the symptoms. To make a certain diagnosis of multiple sclerosis, doctors must do three things:

1 Find evidence of damage to myelin in at least two separate places through the CNS

>   **AND**

2 Find evidence that the damage occurred repeatedly over time, at least one month apart

>   **AND**

3 Rule out any other causes of the symptoms.

Other Causes for Symptoms

Symptoms of multiple sclerosis are caused by loss of myelin. Several other conditions can cause temporary or permanent myelin damage. These include some viral infections, Lyme disease, exposure to heavy metals, vitamin B12 deficiency, and some autoimmune disorders such as AIDS in which the immune system can attack healthy neurons. A condition called Guillain-Barré Syndrome can also cause loss of myelin, but this is in the peripheral nerves and not in the CNS.

Viewing the CNS

The best way to actually see the damage caused by multiple sclerosis in the body is to use magnetic resonance imaging (MRI). This technique uses magnets to view the interior of the CNS.

How It Works

An MRI scanner is a big machine shaped like a tunnel that a person is put into. The scanning process relies on the fact that a powerful magnetic field, the area in which a magnetic force works, can cause water in the body to shift position. It does this by making charged particles in water, called hydrogen protons, line up in the direction of the field. Then radio waves are directed at the protons (positively charged particles) to knock them out of line. Finally, the radio waves are turned off, and the protons relax and line up again in the field. When they relax, the protons vibrate at a speed that the system can detect.

This process has a big effect on the human body, which is around 60 percent water, mostly trapped in cells. An MRI scanner "reads" the water in different human tissues and a computer program converts the data into images. These images show whether the tissues contain normal or abnormal cells, based on their water content.

The tunnel of an MRI scanner can be scary for people with claustrophobia (a fear of tight places). Scan cycles usually take around one hour.

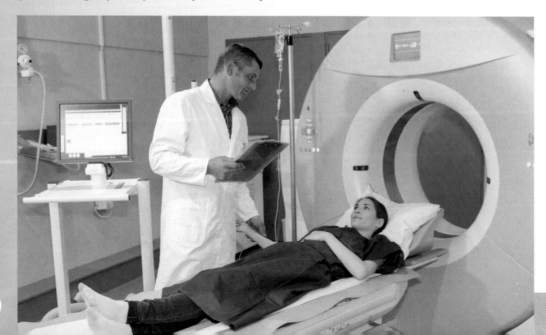

Signs of Multiple Sclerosis

Myelin is a type of fat that repels water. Therefore, areas of tissue that have neurons with less myelin than usual, which is typical of multiple sclerosis plaques, hold onto more water than normal brain and spinal cord tissue. The MRI scanner takes many cross-sectional (slice) images in a session, and can piece them together into a 3D view of the affected area. The results of repeated scan visits can demonstrate the presence of myelin damage in different places and at different times. This can help to confirm the multiple sclerosis diagnosis. MRIs can also be used in progressive forms of the disease to track CNS damage.

On an MRI scan image of a brain with multiple sclerosis, plaques with low myelin and relatively high water usually show up as white spots.

GENE STORIES

"I've had a few scan sessions, so I know the ropes. Ditch your own clothes and any jewelry because anything metal, from zippers to piercings, get attracted to the magnets! Lie on the bed and put a pad under your knees for comfort—it takes a while! Ask for earphones so you can listen to some music, but also to drown out the bumps or buzzes you hear with each scan slice. The more still you stay, the clearer the scans, and the sooner you go home."
— *Darius, age twenty-two*

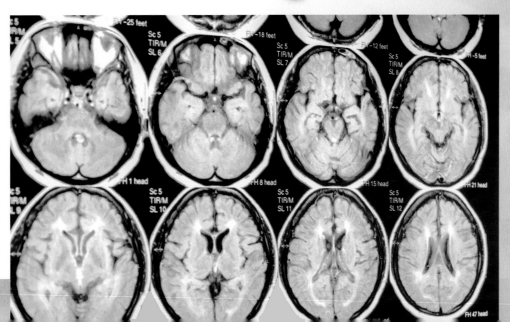

Other Clinical Tests

A series of MRI scans can show myelin damage in people, helping to confirm multiple sclerosis. But in around 5 percent of people already diagnosed with the disease, MRI scans reveal no plaques. Additionally, plaques can be spotted in scans of people over the age of fifty that are a normal sign of aging rather than of multiple sclerosis. Other clinical tests are therefore used to assess changing myelin distribution in different ways without direct visualization.

Lumbar Puncture

A lumbar puncture, or spinal tap, is a produre in which a neurologist inserts a needle into the space around the spinal cord, under local anesthetic. The patient curls up to open a gap between two vertebrae, or spine bones, to do this. Neurologists use a syringe to carefully remove around one or two teaspoons (5–10 milliliters) of cerebrospinal fluid. While doing so, they must take care not to damage the spinal cord. Cerebrospinal fluid is a clear, colorless liquid that circulates around the brain and spinal cord. It normally acts as a shock absorber for the CNS against damage if the skull and vertebrae get knocked. It also circulates nutrients filtered from the blood that CNS cells need to remain healthy, and removes waste products from brain tissue. It may contain other substances as well, some of which can indicate multiple sclerosis.

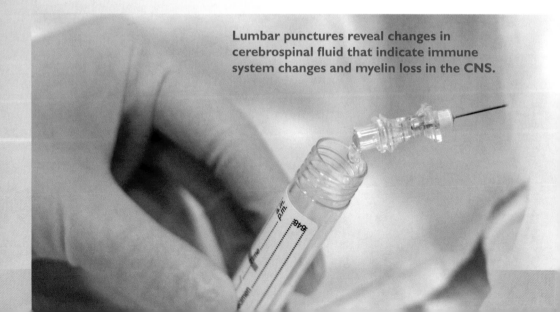

Lumbar punctures reveal changes in cerebrospinal fluid that indicate immune system changes and myelin loss in the CNS.

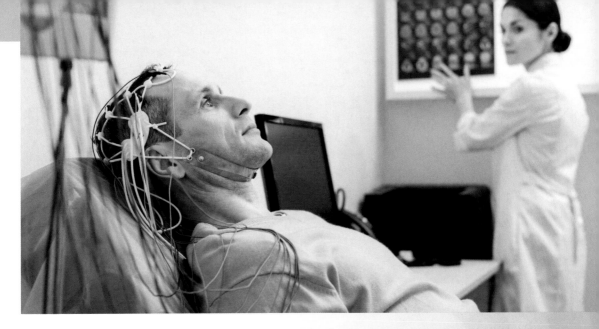

A painless test called evoked potential testing can confirm myelin damage or loss in the optic nerve, which go along with the results from MRI scans.

To detect these substances, the fluid is sent to laboratories for examination by trained workers. In people with multiple sclerosis, the cerebrospinal fluid often shows raised levels of IgG antibodies produced by the body in response to T-cell attack. A test can reveal IgG antibodies of different sizes that indicate inflammation in the CNS. Lumbar puncture samples from people with multiple sclerosis also have raised levels of proteins produced when myelin is damaged by the immune system.

Eye to Brain

Another clinical test measures the time it takes for messages from a patient's eyes to reach his or her brain along the optic nerve. The neurologist places small pads called electrodes on the patient's head over the area of the brain where visual activity takes place. The patient sits in front of a screen that displays a changing checkerboard pattern of light and dark squares. If the optic nerve and CNS are not working normally due to axon myelin problems, the brain reacts more slowly than normal to the visual stimulus of the pattern change. Electrodes record this change as an evoked potential electrical signal.

Chapter 4

Treating Multiple Sclerosis

Some diseases or conditions can be treated quite easily. For example, dracunculiasis is a painful disease caused by a parasitic worm. It has symptoms of intense burning pain, fever, and allergic reactions. It can be avoided by drinking clean water which is free of the worms. The incidence of this disease is very low. Other curable diseases, such as smallpox, have been totally wiped out. Multiple sclerosis cannot be cured like smallpox, but it can be managed using a variety of drug treatments. Doctors and neurologists decide on the best treatments to give, depending on what type of multiple sclerosis a patient has.

Disease Modifying Therapies

Treatments called disease modifying therapies (DMTs) aim to prevent or reduce the number of relapses in relapsing-remitting multiple sclerosis. One class of DMT drugs is called beta-interferons. Your body makes proteins called interferons that reduce inflammation in tissues such as the CNS. Beta-interferons are human-made versions that do the same thing. Different types are mostly injected under the skin, using a fine-needle syringe, once every few days or weeks. Beta-interferons can cause minor side effects such as headaches, muscle aches, or chills, and can reduce the number of relapses and the speed at which a person's disability progresses.

Doctors may prescribe a DMT called alemtuzumab to people with active relapses of their multiple sclerosis. This drug kills T-cells to stop them from damaging the CNS. It can be highly effective for patients, reducing the number of relapses and the severity of the disease by around half. The problem is that alemtuzumab exposes people to infections, especially urinary tract and throat infections; can damage the thyroid gland, which is important in hormone production; and can also cause serious blood problems. Other types of

DMTs include immunosuppressant drugs that hinder cell division, which is the way cells make copies of themselves to increase in number. Immunosuppressants can reduce the number of immune system cells and can be effective in some people with progressive forms of multiple sclerosis.

Symptom Management

Some drug treatments can help patients deal with their symptoms. For example, people may have urinary incontinence because their bladder muscles cannot hold onto urine or empty normally. One treatment is to inject Botox into the bladder wall. This drug is used in cosmetic surgery to reduce wrinkles on people's faces by blocking muscle contractions. Botox can help stop muscles from suddenly emptying the bladder, too. People with mobility problems may be prescribed dalfampridine. This drug blocks tiny holes on exposed axons to help impulses move through them so patients can walk faster.

Steroids are drugs prescribed to reduce inflammation, which is typical in the CNS during relapses in people with multiple sclerosis.

Rehabilitation

Many people with multiple sclerosis face difficulties in their daily lives, from loss of mobility and weakness to incontinence and difficulty swallowing. People with multiple sclerosis have many rehabilitation options to help them take control of their own lives and change them for the better. Rehabilitation means restoring someone's health through different therapies and training.

Improving Mobility

Health care workers called physical therapists help improve the strength, control, and flexibility of patients' arms and legs through resistance exercises that force muscles to contract. For example, they can massage, stretch, and move legs by hand or using gym equipment. This increases the range of movement and prevents joint stiffness. Physical therapists also teach strategies to improve posture and leg position that increase stability when walking. Many people with multiple sclerosis experience foot drop, which is the loss of tone in foot muscles, which makes it difficult to lift their feet properly. Wearing braces or splints helps keep the foot shape stable and reduces the chances of tripping or stumbling. Some people wear a leg band that produces mild electric shocks. This technique, called functional electrical stimulation (FES), produces nerve impulses that contract the foot muscles, reducing foot drop. Physical therapists can also help people choose mobility aids such as rolling walkers and scooters that help them move around when walking is challenging during relapses.

GENE STORIES

"Even though a splint was helping my stability, my leg muscles got thinner and I had bad circulation because walking was tricky. So my physical therapist said why not try this FES? I strapped it on just under my knee, stood up, felt a buzz, looked down, and my foot magically stiffened. It's kind of weird because your brain isn't controlling your feet and you need to train yourself to coordinate strides. I'm not going to take off running anytime soon, but it definitely makes a difference in getting around."

—Terrence, age forty

Speech and swallowing therapists teach people with different muscle abilities how to shape their mouths to improve function in making words or consuming food.

Speech and Swallowing Therapy

If people with multiple sclerosis have plaques in parts of the brain that control speech and swallowing, they may need the help of speech and swallowing therapists. These therapists evaluate patients for their individual needs, identifying specific places from lips to esophagus where changed movement is causing a problem. They may insert flexible, thin cameras called endoscopes to see problem areas inside the throat. Therapists then offer strategies to help, such as exercises that strengthen neck muscles. A stronger neck enables a patient to hold the head more upright to swallow better and avoid choking.

Feeling Well

The right diet, exercise, and other healthy behaviors can make anyone feel well, and this is no different for people with multiple sclerosis.

Diet

There is no special multiple sclerosis diet. However, like everyone else, people with multiple sclerosis can change their energy level, digestive function, and overall health by eating well. Doctors recommend a diet high in fiber and low in fat, rich in vegetables and fruit, with less sugar and salt. A diet supplemented with omega-3 fatty acids from oily fish, cod-liver oil, and flaxseed oil, along with omega-6 fatty acids from sunflower oil, may improve myelin production. Vitamin D supplements benefit the CNS and immune system. However, individuals need to consult their doctors before taking them because they can worsen certain heart conditions and increase kidney stones in some people.

Avoid Smoking

Smoking tobacco has long been known to cause lung cancer and heart disease, but is now understood to worsen symptoms in people with multiple sclerosis. Every additional year of smoking

Oily fish such as mackerel can form part of a healthy diet for people with multiple sclerosis.

after a multiple sclerosis diagnosis can speed up the shift to secondary-progressive multiple sclerosis by nearly 5 percent. Smokers with multiple sclerosis have a higher risk of relapse, more plaques on MRI, and greater disability. One possible reason is that smoking raises the risk of infections, thus stimulating more immune system activity.

Exercise

When anyone does not exercise sufficiently, they face an increased risk of health issues ranging from weakness and shallow breathing, to becoming overweight and having heart problems. People with multiple sclerosis who exercise often see physical improvements such as increased strength, better bladder and bowel control, and less fatigue. Exercise in water is especially helpful, partly because a person's buoyancy (ability to float) supports his or her weight so movement takes less effort. Resistance to movement from water can be used to increase strength and practice balance and coordination without falling.

Developing core and limb strength through exercise helps mobility in people with multiple sclerosis.

Alternatives

Some people with multiple sclerosis find that their symptoms improve after using complementary and alternative treatments. These are treatments whose effects are generally unproven by conventional scientific knowledge. One such treatment is acupuncture, where thin needles are pushed into the skin at particular locations. Another is magnetic field therapy, which uses strong magnetic pulses to stimulate charged particles in cells, and which some people claim reduces pain and inflammation. People may practice yoga and tai chi to increase mobility and calmness, too.

Chapter 5

Living with Multiple Sclerosis

Living with any life-altering disease is a challenge. Part of the challenge with multiple sclerosis is the changing nature of the symptoms, along with the relapses and progressions which are part of the disease. Most people will experience increasing disability and difficulty carrying out daily tasks. Facing any challenge alone is not easy, so it really helps people with the disease to have a support network.

Support Network

This network includes family doctors, neurologists, physical therapists, and other health care professionals. These professionals can alter therapies depending on the changing needs of the patient over time. However, they cannot be present all the time, so another key part of the support network is the caregiver. Some people can pay for home helpers who may assist, for example, with getting groceries, helping with pills, cooking meals, cleaning the home, washing clothes, or helping the person to bathe. However, many people rely on unpaid caregivers to help with such activities. These caregivers may be friends or family members such as spouses, siblings, or children. They may have a formal or informal arrangement, fitting caregiving around childcare, work, or college.

Support groups are also part of the support network for people with multiple sclerosis. There are many networks of fellow sufferers who meet up online or in person at halls, hospitals, or colleges. These groups can be a great help for people to share tips on dealing with symptoms of the disease and to talk about the challenges, successes, and frustrations of life with multiple sclerosis.

Occupational Therapy

Occupational therapists are another important element of the support network. Their job is to make it easier for people with multiple sclerosis to go about their daily activities, ranging from washing and dressing to cooking and taking part in leisure activities. For example, installing ramps and widening doors in a home can make it easier for someone with multiple sclerosis to move their mobility scooter around. Grab rails and seats can make it safer for them to lower themselves onto the toilet or take a shower by themselves. Adding a walk-in shower rather than a regular shower or tub to a home can make washing easier. For people who struggle to hold regular utensils, specially designed utensils with easy-to-grip, larger handles and angled tips may allow them to feed themselves more easily.

Occupational therapists can teach people how to be confident in the use of wheelchairs so they can continue to live their regular lives.

Life's Hurdles

There are many daily hurdles that people with multiple sclerosis have to overcome. For example, it can be tricky and slow to walk unaided or using canes, crutches, or mobility scooters, so many journeys need to be planned in advance with extra time allowed to reach destinations. Two particular challenges for people with multiple sclerosis involve incontinence and overheating.

Incontinence

Incontinence, or the experience of wetting or soiling yourself, can be embarrassing. It should not be—after all, incontinence is at least an occasional problem for around one in seven women in the United States. Some people with incontinence resulting from multiple sclerosis use catheters, or tubes into their urethras (urinary tracts), so they can empty their urine into a toilet or into bags they may wear under their clothing. Using catheters can help people control the emptying of their bladder, but they can also increase the chances of getting urinary infections. These infections cause painful inflammation and may require antibiotics. Other people rely on getting to the toilet in time, but often have little warning that they will need to go. There are various strategies to help reduce stress related to incontinence:

- Plan frequent stops and know the location of easily accessible toilets when out of the house.

- Wear an incontinence pad that can absorb the urine or stool (solid waste) without soaking clothes.

- Wear pants that can easily be taken off, such as pants with an elastic waistband.

- Carry a spare set of underwear, pads, catheters, and other incontinence-related needs at all times.

- Drink lots of water to reduce constipation. Doing this might increase the frequency of restroom trips, but this is better than having concentrated urine that can lead to more painful urinary infections.

Heat Effects

Heat worsens the symptoms for many people with multiple sclerosis without actually causing more loss of myelin or nerve damage. Once the temperature drops, the symptoms improve. Some people with the disease who live in warm places make the big change of moving somewhere with a cooler climate. However, there are many less-drastic options for dealing with heat effects. These include wearing lightweight, loose-fitting clothing made of natural fibers such as cotton; being active at cooler times of the day; installing air conditioning or fans to cool room interiors on hot days; and taking long, cooling baths to lower the body temperature when overheating becomes a problem.

Heating up through exercise can make anyone feel uncomfortable, but can badly aggravate symptoms in those with multiple sclerosis.

Difficult Changes

During the course of life with multiple sclerosis, and progression in their symptoms, people face many difficult changes.

Changing Mood

Shifting moods and thoughts are common in multiple sclerosis and may include:

Grief: People may feel incredible sadness when they have poor mobility and little energy to do things. They may feel they have lost the person they once thought they were.

Anxiety: People may worry about future unpredictability of symptoms, loss of independence, or even loss of employment. One survey of people with multiple sclerosis found that around 80 percent of respondents had to give up work within fifteen years of diagnosis due to difficult symptoms.

Exercise can help people with multiple sclerosis to manage the stress associated with the disorder.

Depression: People may face long periods of very low moods during which they feel terribly sad, cut-off, and sometimes even suicidal. Depression is never normal or acceptable, and it needs professional help just as much as any serious physical symptom would.

Cognitive changes: Around half of all people with multiple sclerosis experience difficulties with memory, problem-solving, and concentration.

Feelings of grief, depression, and loss are also common among close family members seeing the great changes in their loved ones who have the disease.

Managing Stress

Stress can feel overwhelming for people with the unpredictable symptoms and uncertain future of multiple sclerosis. People can use strategies to help manage stress, such as treating challenges as opportunities for creative problem-solving and demonstrating resilience against the disease. They can prioritize things that make them feel healthy and well, such as favorite hobbies, taking part in group sports, relaxing, and spending quality time with family and friends. Building and nurturing close relationships provides opportunities to share experiences and goals, solve problems together, and enjoy mutual support. People can also manage stress by avoiding behaviors that make them feel worse, such as overdoing strenuous activity, not getting enough sleep, eating unhealthy foods, taking drugs, or drinking alcohol.

Family support and quality time together are important factors in the happiness of many people with multiple sclerosis.

GENE STORIES

"I take advantage of any modern technology that helps make my life easier and more independent, because my limbs have limited movement nowadays. Like the hands-free control for my wheelchair and its computer. It is pretty cool when I turn on lights, open doors, and use my mobile phone at the nod of my head. And people are amazed when my chair can raise up, so we can meet eye to eye. It really helps us relate on the same level, rather than being looked down on all the time."

—*Irene, age fifty-five*

Chapter 6

Multiple Sclerosis and Gene Therapy

Scientists studying cells from thousands of patients with multiple sclerosis have identified more than a hundred genes that are involved in the disease. The hope in the future is that scientists will be able to replace mutations with normal copies of genes to help prevent or cure the condition. This type of treatment is called gene therapy.

How Gene Therapy Works

The most common gene therapy method uses modified viruses to transport replacement sections of DNA into chromosomes in cells. Scientists in a laboratory remove any of the virus's own genes that could cause sicknesses in people. They then replace them with the normal functioning gene to be added in the gene therapy procedure. The viruses then enter cells and "infect" them with the normal gene, replacing the mutated gene. The corrected cells are injected into the patient to replace faulty cells and spread copies of the normal gene.

Problems for Multiple Sclerosis

In diseases such as cystic fibrosis, a single, identified gene mutation is responsible. The idea of using gene therapy in such situations is reasonable. However, multiple sclerosis is much more complicated, partly because it involves many genes as possible mutation sites. But those genes interact

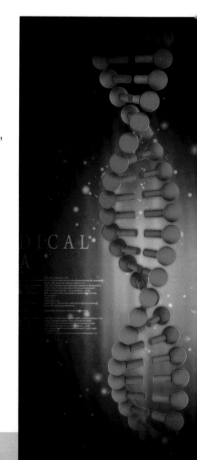

The chemical codes in DNA, form of genes, are the instruc books of our bodies.

Gene Genies

Scientists at the University of Florida have been testing a possible gene therapy for multiple sclerosis on mice. They injected modified viruses carrying the normal copy of a gene responsible for myelin production in the brain into their livers. The liver is part of the body's immune system, acting as a kind of school to educate T-cells that regulate immune attacks by other T-cells. They hope that if the liver can recognize the virus as harmless, it will spark production of T-cells that suppress attacks on cells making myelin in the CNS.

in complex ways, and are only activated after particular environmental triggers, such as vitamin D levels. In addition, a problem common to most gene therapy is that introduced cells containing viruses can be recognized as intruders and be attacked by a patient's immune system. In the CNS, introduced neurons might trigger increased T-cell attack, with greater loss of myelin and worsening of symptoms. Despite these obstacles, scientists are carefully studying the activities of different genes in search of key genes that might be suitable for gene therapy in the future.

Scientists at the University of Florida have been testing a possible gene therapy for multiple sclerosis on mice.

Stem Cell Therapy

Researchers are exploring whether it is possible to introduce new cells into people with multiple sclerosis to slow their disease activity, repair existing damage, or replace faulty parts of the nervous or immune systems. This therapy is not yet available for multiple sclerosis. But it is already in use to treat conditions such as leukemia, or cancer of the blood.

What Are Stem Cells?

Muscles contain muscle cells, some of which can change shape to allow muscle contraction and relaxation. Intestines are lined with cells that absorb nutrients from digested food into the blood. Red blood cells carry oxygen to other cells for respiration. These cells and most other cells in the body are specialized with very specific functions. Some cells, however, are unspecialized. Called stem cells, they have the potential to develop into one of a number of different specialized cell types, depending on the body's needs at a particular time. They are part of the body's normal repair system and are found in the CNS, bone marrow, blood, and other body sites.

One of the great things about stem cells is that they can make copies of themselves. Most specialized cells cannot do this, but one stem cell can split over and over to produce millions of cells over many months. This can be made to happen in glass dishes in laboratories, not just inside a human body. Scientists speed up the process by adding chemicals in a growth solution so stem cells divide more quickly. Then they can make lots of copies of the stem cells that they need in therapies.

Stem Cell Strategies

In the future, doctors and neurologists may be able to offer stem cell therapy to replace faulty, damaged, or missing cells in the immune system or in the CNS. There are several experimental strategies. One uses cells in bone marrow, or in the fat layer beneath the skin, to protect CNS cells from disease processes and to promote repair. But the strategy that has been studied, the most and that is currently in trial, is very drastic. It involves completely rebooting the immune system so it no longer attacks the brain and spinal cord to cause further damage. This is called autologous hematopoietic stem cell transplantation, or AHSCT. AHSCT uses powerful drugs to wipe out harmful cells in the immune system of a patient with multiple sclerosis. It then rebuilds a new immune system using stem cells previously collected from their blood.

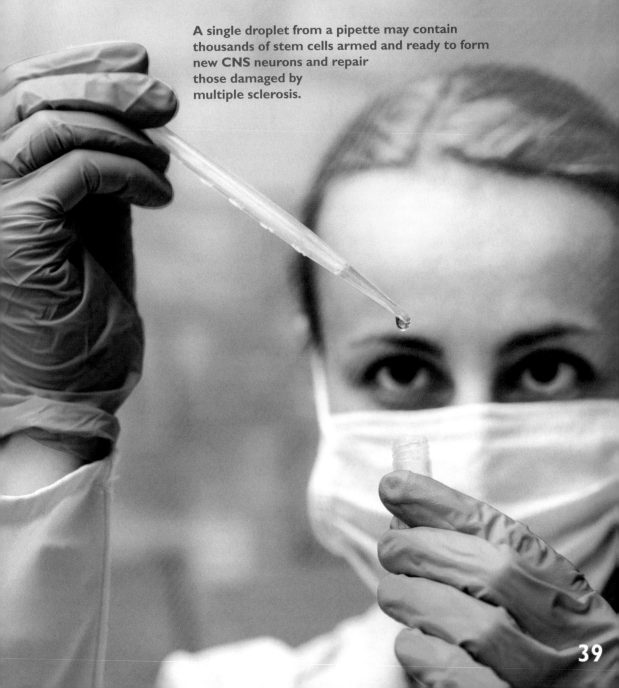

A single droplet from a pipette may contain thousands of stem cells armed and ready to form new CNS neurons and repair those damaged by multiple sclerosis.

How It Works

The AHSCT procedure is complex and involves several steps. It is risky for patients. Doctors recommend it mostly for people with relapsing multiple sclerosis in which there is active inflammation of the CNS, rather than for those with significant disability and progressive forms of the disease.

Step 1 – Mobilization: The blood only contains a small number of stem cells naturally, but many are needed for AHSCT. So the first step is to encourage stem cells to increase in number and move from the bone marrow into the blood. This is done using drugs delivered into a patient's veins through a drip and injections.

Step 2 – Harvesting: After about ten days, the patient has a blood test to confirm there are enough stem cells. Then a needle is put in patient's arm and attached to a cell separator machine. Blood circulates through the machine as it separates out the stem cells and returns the rest of the blood to the patient's body. The harvested stem cells are then frozen until they are to be transplanted back into the patient in a hospital.

Step 3 – Chemotherapy: The use of strong drugs to kill cells is called chemotherapy. It is often used in cancer treatment to kill cancer cells. In AHSCT, chemotherapy is used to destroy the T-cells and other immune system cells involved in multiple sclerosis. Patients must stay in a hospital for several days while they receive chemotherapy.

Patients undergoing AHSCT have their stem cells harvested before their bodies' immune systems are wiped out in preparation for the stem cells' return.

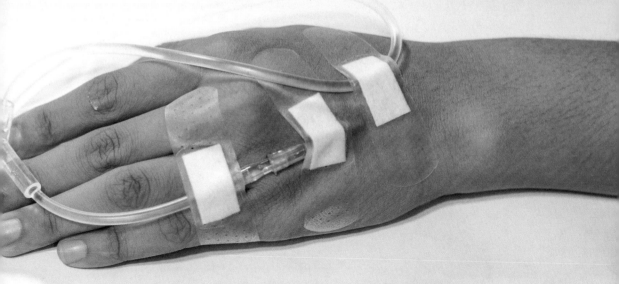

Chemotherapy is often given through a needle into a socket fixed into a vein in the hand.

Step 4 – Transplantation: After the chemotherapy is complete, and any traces of the drug have cleared from the patient's blood, the stored stem cells are thawed and returned to the patient's blood through a drip. This takes a couple of hours. After that, it can take up to thirty days for the stem cells to enter the patient's bone marrow and start to make new blood and immune system cells. These cells should not attack the patient's CNS.

Risky

After chemotherapy and transplantation, a patient is very susceptible to infection because they have a much-weakened immune system. They have to stay in an isolation room in a hospital. Health care workers keep visitors away and give drugs immediately to treat any infections the patient might develop from viruses already in his or her system. If infections get out of hand, they can rapidly become life threatening. Patients may also need drugs to treat side effects of chemotherapy, such as nausea, vomiting, and bleeding. Even after their new immune system is up and running, patients feel weak and lack energy. They may take up to a year to recover.

Repairing the CNS

One possible future stem cell therapy is to repair the damaged CNS tissue of people with multiple sclerosis. Although an exciting idea, it is far from becoming reality. However, other therapies will soon be available to help the CNS repair itself more effectively.

Introducing Healthier Oligodendrocytes

Stem cell treatment for myelin repair will probably use something called induced pluripotent stem cells, which are specialized cells reprogrammed in laboratories to behave like stem cells. These stem cells could be used to grow enhanced oligodendrocytes that can suppress immune attack and make lots of myelin. They could then be injected into the CNS to massively increase its potential to make more myelin.

Improving Myelin Repair

Oligodendrocytes form from brain stem cells called oligodendrocyte precursor cells (OPCs). Neurons release chemical signals as a "cry for help" when their myelin is damaged. When the signals reach the OPCs, they travel to the site of damage, such as a growing plaque,

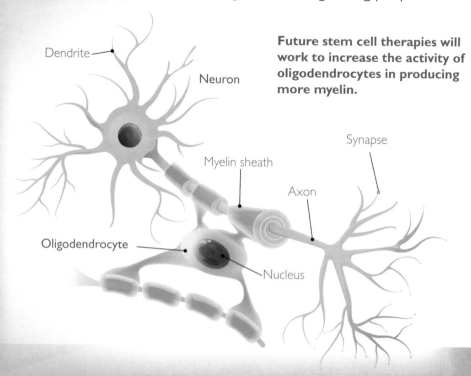

Future stem cell therapies will work to increase the activity of oligodendrocytes in producing more myelin.

Dendrite

Neuron

Synapse

Myelin sheath

Axon

Oligodendrocyte

Nucleus

then transform into mature cells that can produce myelin. Researchers are examining alternative treatments and drugs that can enhance this process in patients with multiple sclerosis so they can naturally repair their own myelin more effectively. Some of the possible treatments include:

Biotin: A vitamin that activates enzymes in the CNS that help the growth of OPCs into oligodendrocytes and boost their myelin production.

Clemastine: An antihistamine used to relieve itching in people with chicken pox and eczema. This antihistamine enters the brain and causes drowsiness, but it also suppresses the activity of T-cells. In people with multiple sclerosis, this could reduce immune system damage to myelin.

Anti-LINGO-1: An antibody that blocks the activity of a protein found in neurons and oligodendrocytes, resulting in myelin repair. In a trial in 2015, Anti-LINGO-1 was injected into the optic nerves of volunteers with optic neuritis. Their evoked potential test results were improved over volunteers injected with a liquid without the antibody in it.

Other medications with the potential for myelin repair are best known for other uses. One such medication, tamoxifen, is usually prescribed to treat breast cancer. Another, miconazole, is commonly used to treat athlete's foot!

Gene Genies

Scientists at Cambridge University in the United Kingdom identified a vitamin D receptor protein on oligodendrocytes. When activated by vitamin D, the receptor works with another protein to boost myelin production. In a laboratory, blocking the receptor reduced myelin production by around 80 percent. In the future, they believe a myelin repair drug targeting this receptor could help people with multiple sclerosis.

Hope for the Future

There is great hope for future treatment of multiple sclerosis. Gene therapy is very experimental and stem cell therapy is in its infancy. Yet both are exciting possibilities for treating the disease and lessening its symptoms. One day soon, perhaps these will be used with well-established drug and rehabilitation therapies. However, life with multiple sclerosis is difficult. That's why there is always new research with the hope of improving the lives of people with multiple sclerosis.

Research Alliance

Scientists, neurologists, and epidemiologists working for charities, research institutions, and hospitals are searching for, testing, and ensuring the safety of new treatments. Many of the charities are part of the Progressive MS Alliance. This is a global network of charities united in speeding up diagnosis, monitoring, and developing treatments for progressive multiple sclerosis. Up to now, it has been trickier to diagnose quickly and to treat than the relapsing form.

Promising New Treatments

Here are a few recent ideas that might be put to use in the future:

Neuroprotection: The aim of neuroprotection is to keep neurons alive and active, even if their myelin is damaged. One class of drugs, called sodium channel blockers, prevent the buildup of sodium (salt) in the brain that is linked with nerve damage. A 2016 trial using a sodium channel blocker called phenytoin, which is often used to treat epilepsy, showed that its use reduced damage to the optic nerve by 30 percent during optic neuritis.

Immunomodulators: Several new disease modifying treatments called immunomodulators are showing promise in targeting the specific immune system cells that appear to control the shift from relapsing to progressive multiple sclerosis. For example, in a 2016 trial, a drug called siponimod reduced disability progression by 21 percent in volunteers with secondary-progressive multiple sclerosis. It also reduced shrinking of brain tissue caused by widespread plaques.

Gene Genies

Investigators from The International Multiple Sclerosis Microbiome Study are collecting stool samples from people with multiple sclerosis. Their aim is to identify the types and numbers of bacteria the stools contain. The stomach and intestines contain millions of bacteria that are thought to be extremely important in establishing and maintaining immune balance in people. The feeling is that certain species of bacteria may protect people from multiple sclerosis, but others may cause immune attack on the CNS and put them at risk of developing the disease. If multiple sclerosis bacteria are found, it may be possible to manipulate bacteria populations in people with the disease to make them healthier.

Researchers are getting closer to perfecting treatments to keep neurons communicating and to battle autoimmune attack. Someday, people with progressive multiple sclerosis will face fewer symptoms of the disease.

Glossary

AHSCT Type of stem cell therapy to treat relapsing multiple sclerosis.

antibodies Blood proteins that stop invaders from entering the body.

bladder Muscular bag storing urine in the lower abdomen.

bone marrow The mushy core of bones, where blood cells are made.

Botox Poison used in controlled amounts to stop muscles from contracting.

central nervous system (CNS) Brain and spinal cord.

chromosomes Parts of a cell that contain genes.

constipation Hard stools, or difficulty emptying the bowels.

coordination Ability to use different parts of the body together smoothly and efficiently.

depression Serious medical illness that negatively affects how people feel, the way they think, and how they act.

diagnosis Process of identifying an illness or condition.

disease modifying treatments (DMTs) Treatments that slow a disease's progression.

epidemiologists Experts in the distribution, incidence, and control of diseases.

esophagus Inside part of the throat.

ethnic group Group of people with a distinct historic and ideological identity.

evoked potential Electrical response of nerves following external stimulus.

genes Cell parts that control or influence the way a person looks, grows, and develops.

gene therapy The process of replacing genes in cells to correct genetic disorders.

impulses Movements of electrical signals through the nervous system.

incontinence Loss of control over one's urination or defecation.

infections Kinds of diseases usually caused by bacteria or viruses that can often be caught from other people.

inherit Get from a parent.

magnetic resonance imaging (MRI) An imaging process that uses magnets to form digital pictures of the inside of the body.

migrate Permanently move from one country to another.

mutations Significant changes in the structure of a gene.

myelin Fatty substance that insulates axons, helping them transmit impulses.

nervous system The network of nerve cells and fibers that transmits nerve impulses between parts of the body.

oligodendrocytes Cells in the CNS that produce myelin.

optic neuritis Inflammation of the optic nerve.

peripheral In the surrounding area; peripheral nerves are found through the outer parts of the body.

physical therapists People who help patients improve their moblity through movement and exercise.

plaques Areas of damaged neurons in the CNS.

progressive Taking place or changing gradually, often getting worse over time.

reflexes Physical action that you cannot control, such as pulling away from hot objects..

rehabilitation The use of training and therapy to restore or improve health.

resilience Ability to bounce back or quickly recover.

specialized Modified for a particular function.

spinal cord Major nerve connecting peripheral nerves and the brain.

stem cells Cells that can divide many times to produce more stem cells and also can turn into different types of cells.

symptoms Changes in the body or mind caused by a disease or health condition.

T-cell A type of white blood cell important in the immune system for finding and destroying invaders.

unspecialized Not modified for a particular function.

vitamin D Essential vitamin mostly formed naturally through exposure to sunlight; important for good health.

For Further Reading

Brill, Marlene Targ. *Chronic Illnesses, Syndromes, and Rare Disorders*. Lanham, MD: Rowman & Littlefield, 2016.

Kalb, Rosalind C. *Multiple Sclerosis: The Questions You Have, the Answers You Need*. New York, NY: Demos Medical Publishing, 2012.

Lyons, David, with Jacob Sloane. *Everyday Health and Fitness with Multiple Sclerosis: Achieve Your Peak Physical Wellness While Working with Limited Mobility*. Beverly, MA: Fair Winds Press, 2017.

Murray, T. Jock. *Multiple Sclerosis: A Guide for the Newly Diagnosed*. New York, NY: Demos Medical Publishing, 2017.

Oelschlager, Vanita. *The Electrifying Story of Multiple Sclerosis*. Akron, OH: Vanita Books, 2015.

Stachowiak, Julie. *The Multiple Sclerosis Manifesto: Action to Take, Principles to Live By*. New York, NY: Demos Health, 2010.

Index